CHICKEN

David M. Schwartz is an award-winning author of children's books, on a wide variety of topics, loved by children around the world. Dwight Kuhn's scientific expertise and artful eye work together with the camera to capture the awesome wonder of the natural world.

Please visit our web site at: www.garethstevens.com
For a free color catalog describing Gareth Stevens Publishing's list of high-quality books
and multimedia programs, call 1-800-542-2595 (USA) or 1-800-461-9120 (Canada).
Gareth Stevens Publishing's Fax: (414) 332-3567.

Library of Congress Cataloging-in-Publication Data

Schwartz, David M.
    Chicken / by David M. Schwartz; photographs by Dwight Kuhn. — North American ed.
       p. cm. — (Life cycles: a springboards into science series)
    Includes bibliographical references and index.
    ISBN 0-8368-2971-9 (lib. bdg.)
    1. Chickens—Life cycles—Juvenile literature. [1. Chickens.] I. Kuhn, Dwight, ill.
II. Title.
SF487.5.S435   2001
598.6'25—dc21   2001031464

This North American edition first published in 2001 by
Gareth Stevens Publishing
A World Almanac Education Group Company
330 West Olive Street, Suite 100
Milwaukee, WI 53212 USA

First published in the United States in 1999 by Creative Teaching Press, Inc., P.O. Box 2723, Huntington Beach, CA 92647-0723.
Text © 1999 by David M. Schwartz; photographs © 1999 by Dwight Kuhn. Additional end matter © 2001 by Gareth Stevens, Inc.

Gareth Stevens editor: Mary Dykstra

Printed in the United States of America

1 2 3 4 5 6 7 8 9 05 04 03 02 01

CHICKEN

by David M. Schwartz

photographs by Dwight Kuhn

A SPRINGBOARDS INTO
SCIENCE
SERIES

Gareth Stevens Publishing
A WORLD ALMANAC EDUCATION GROUP COMPANY

Many farms have chickens strutting around the barnyard. There are many kinds of chickens. These are white leghorns. The male leghorn is bigger than the female and has longer tail feathers, too. The male is called a rooster. The female is called a hen.

A hen lays eggs, even if there is no rooster around. If a hen mates with a rooster, he fertilizes her eggs. A chick will grow inside each fertilized egg.

After a hen lays several eggs, she begins to brood, or sit on the eggs to keep them warm. A brooding hen never leaves her eggs for very long.

7

A chick begins as a tiny spot on the yolk of an egg. Within a few days, a body and a tail form. The developing chick, called an embryo, gets food from the yolk. The embryo also gets some food and lots of water from the egg white.

The embryo grows quickly. After two weeks, it has feathers. About a week later, cheeping sounds come from the egg. The chick is ready to hatch!

9

The chick uses a special egg tooth on its beak to poke a hole through the eggshell. Then it slowly chips away the shell all the way around the egg. For a tiny chick, hatching is a big job!

Finally, the little bird pushes the shell apart.
Out comes the chick, weak and wet.

At first, young chicks stay close to their mother. They snuggle under her to keep warm. Their bodies are covered with soft feathers, called down.

In a day or two, chicks begin to walk and peck the ground, looking for grain and other food.

In two to three weeks, new feathers begin to replace a chick's soft down. The chick is growing up, and it starts to spend more and more time away from its mother.

In just five months, a young hen is ready to start laying eggs.

All chickens squawk and cluck, but roosters are the loudest of all. At dawn, a rooster puffs out his chest and crows as loudly as he can. He seems to be telling the world how important he is!

Roosters are important.
They mate with hens so
that a new generation
of chickens can be born.

Can you put these steps in the life cycle of a chicken in order?

Answer

brood (v): sit on eggs to keep them warm until they hatch.

dawn: the first light of daytime; sunrise.

down: the fine, fluffy feathers on baby birds or under the outer feathers of older birds.

egg tooth: a sharp point on the beak of an unhatched bird that is used to break through the eggshell.

embryo: the first stage of growth in the life of a plant or animal.

fertilizes: brings male and female cells together so a new plant or animal can grow.

generation: all of the young that are born during a particular time period.

grain: the small, hard seeds of plants such as wheat and corn.

hatch: come, or break, out of an egg.

leghorns: chickens belonging to a breed, or kind, that is known for laying large quantities of white eggs.

mates (v): joins male or female cells together to produce young.

peck: poke at with a pointed object, such as a bird's beak.

strutting: walking in a proud way to show off or attract attention.

yolk: the part of an egg that contains food for a developing baby animal.

ACTIVITIES

Hair-Raising Fun

Wash out and carefully dry some eggshells that are about two-thirds whole. Pretending that the open part of each shell is the top of a head, use felt-tip markers to add eyes, noses, and other features to make faces on the shells. Put some damp cotton inside each shell and sprinkle cress or mustard seeds on it. Place the shells in a sunny spot, adding water, as needed, to keep the cotton moist. Soon your "egg-head" will be very hairy!

Something to Crow About

Roosters crow, pigeons coo, cardinals sing — and you can, too! Listen to a tape or CD of bird songs and try to imitate your favorites. While listening to the recording, look in a bird book to find pictures of and more information about the birds you are hearing.

Eggs-citing Eggs

All birds lay eggs, but some bird eggs are larger than others, and some are more colorful. You can create colorful eggs of your own. Have an adult hard-boil some white chicken eggs for you. After the eggs cool, wrap rubber bands around them to create interesting designs. Then dip the eggs in different colors of food dye. When the colored eggs are completely dry, remove the rubber bands to see your eggs-citing designs.

Can You Tell Who's Who?

Make a chart listing the ways that the roosters and hens in this book look different. Then use a bird book to see the differences between males and females of other bird species. What are the most common differences? List them on your chart. Now go bird-watching and try to tell which birds are males and which are females.

More Books to Read

Animals and Their Eggs. Animals Up Close (series). Renne (Gareth Stevens)

Chickens. Animals Growing and Changing (series). Gail Saunders-Smith (Pebble Books)

Chickens Have Chicks. Animals and Their Young (series). Lynn M. Stone (Compass Point Books)

Egg: A Photographic Story of Hatching. Robert Burton (DK Publishing)

Egg to Chick. Millicent Selsam (Econo-Clad Books)

Inside an Egg. Sylvia A. Johnson (Lerner)

Videos

Baby Animals at Play: Babies of the Barnyard. (Madacy)

Barnyard Babies. (Kimbo Educational)

See How They Grow: Farm Animals. (Sony Music)

Web Sites

chickscope.beckman.uiuc.edu/explore/embryology/

lenoir.ces.state.nc.us/staff/jnix/pubs/an.workbook/chickens.html

www.poultryclub.org/Hatch.htm

Some web sites stay current longer than others. For additional web sites, use a good search engine to locate the following topics: *chickens, fowl, incubation, leghorns,* and *poultry.*

INDEX